236
Mal

# RUSSIA'S
# LAST INVASION

1379

D1515797

# Foreword

It finally began to happen! How else could it develop? Since 1948, when Israel reappeared as a new nation on the world horizon, all who knew their Bible and believed in it received a strong confirmation of their faith; namely, that prophecy thousands of years old were being fulfilled.

Thus, the enemies the Bible speaks of and calls them by name had to appear, such as Persia (Iran), Libya, Ethiopia, East Germany, and especially Russia [Compare Ezekiel 38:5,6]. The closest circles of Israel's neighbors are the Ishmalites, which in their militant, Islamic revolution go to extremes to express their hatred of Israel. And today we are seeing an even greater enemy arising, namely, the anti-Godly nations. By far the greatest enemy will be the anti-Christian nations and today they too begin to raise their ugly heads of anti-Semitism against Israel.

One thing is clear today, the anti-God nation, that is, Russia, has begun its march toward Israel exactly as described by the prophet Ezekiel, Joel, and Jeremiah. This is in no way a battle of interest between the Russians and the Americans or between Communism and Islam. But it is more of a continuous and climaxing conflict of the power of darkness against the Lord and His anointed [Psalm 2:2].

Today, we are witnesses of Russia's ultimate goal, and according to the Word of God, also Russia's final judgment of God in Israel. Russia's intention and God's judgment are the contents of this book. While we attempt to shed light on the world-shaking events in the Middle East, we must hold ourselves to the prophetic Word, for only this prophetic Word and its fulfillment will be the perfect explanation of things or events happening now, and of things to come. Israel is the means to fulfill God's highest goal, namely the revelation of Jesus Christ and His coming in great power and glory with His saints, but in regard to how it exactly will happen we must confess that our knowledge is limited about God's ways and means, for the Bible states, "Eye hath not seen, nor ear heard, neither has entered into the heart of man, the things which God has prepared for them that love Him [I Corinthians 2:9]. However, it is exciting that in our days, we are actually witnessing the things which the Lord Jesus had prophesied to happen before His coming. Thus, we know that our Lord is coming soon! Please read this book with your Bible, so when Jesus comes you will be ready, too!

# RUSSIA'S
## LAST INVASION

Wim Malgo

## Soviet Invasion of Afghanistan

They came during Christmas of 1979, in the same way Vietnam's troops marched into Cambodia the year before, but the entire operation of invasion was based on the Prague plan. That was when Russia invaded Czechoslovakia.

In approximately 200 landings, Soviet Military transport planes landed on December 24th, 25th, and 26th in 1979 at the military airport in Bagram, approximately 80 kilometers north of the capital city, Kabul. They also landed openly at the International Airport in Kabul under the witnessing eyes of international passengers.

Modern tanks and sophisticated weapons rolled out of gigantic airplanes, which included about 5,000 highly trained Soviet military personnel. This action instantly doubled the military advisors in Afghanistan to one full division. A further division was flown in by air and placed in another location.

Simultaneously, on the Soviet Afghanistan border, another five Soviet divisions marched towards Afghanistan according to U.S. Satellite Intelligence.

All roads to the airport of the capital city were closed. The only movement seen was that of Soviet troops in all of Kabul. At exactly 7:30 PM on December 27th, street fights erupted. Some resistance was reported during the occupation of the president's palace and the radio station. Military personnel, faithful to the former government, were arrested. Two Afghanistan tanks were put out of action and at exactly 11:00 PM, the Soviet army had Kabul under control and were patrolling the streets of that city.

For the first time since the Soviet attack of Japan in August of 1945, the Soviet Army was actively fighting outside of its borders, following in the footsteps of the expansion policy once desired by the Czar.

## Why Is The Soviet Union Approaching, Unhinderingly, The Persian Gulf And Coming Closer To Israel?

Obviously, it is the OIL, we answer. This response is certainly true for an impulsive answer, but it does not fit at all into the strategy of Russia. Because of its very carefully built and tenderly developed detente, which was to build a fog-screen in the eyes of the West, it has collapsed together with the invasion of Afghanistan. Because of its long and careful negotiation, for several years now, on SALT II with America, the ratification has been placed in an extremely dangerous position. They also have even lost their trustworthiness towards Socialist Europe. Moreover, Russia is risking a nuclear confrontation with the United States of America.

Therefore, we must ask again, "What in reality is pushing this Communist power towards the South?" Only the Bible gives us a precise answer in Ezekiel 38:3, *"Thus saith the Lord God; Behold, I am against thee, O Gog, the chief prince of Meshech and Tubal: And I will turn thee back, and put hooks into thy jaws, and I will bring thee forth, and all thine army . . . Persia, Ethiopia, and Libya with them . . . Gomer, and all his bands; the house of Togarmah of the north quarters, and all his bands: and many people with thee . . . After many days thou shalt be visited: in the latter years thou shalt come into the land that is brought back from the sword, and is gathered out of many people, against the mountains of Israel, which have been always waste: but it is brought forth out of the na-tions. . . .*" This is the actual reason which is urging the Soviet Union, with its satellite countries, towards its own judgment in Israel. The careful observers recognize that the Russian move towards the Persian Gulf and Israel is rapidly being accelerated in our days. Why is that so? Because, the re-establishment of Israel has become a fact and this fact established another; namely, the rapture of the Church of Jesus. It is standing at our door.

Listen to what The Song of Solomon is prophetically saying in Chapter 2:13, 15 *"the fig tree putteth forth her green figs, and the vines with the tender grape give a good smell . . . Take us the foxes, the little foxes, that spoil the vines: for our vines have tender grapes."* And the Lord Jesus said, *"Now learn a parable of the fig tree; When his branch is yet tender, and putteth forth leaves, ye know that summer is nigh: So likewise ye, when ye shall see all these things, know that it is near, even at the doors"* (Matthew 24:32-33).

## The Year of Redemption

The entire Bible speaks either directly or prophetically about the great event; namely, the year of the redemption of Israel and the Church of Jesus. Both of these organs of salvation we have just seen in The Song of Solomon in Chapter 2:13, 15; namely, Israel as the fig tree, and the Church, as the vine.

The spirit of prophecy is present through the entire Holy Scriptures. All of the heroes of faith saw the redemption afar off and were persuaded by them (Hebrews 11:13). In the same way, all born-again believers who belong to the Church of Jesus have this spirit of prophecy, because this spirit of prophecy is the testimony of Jesus (compare Revelation 19:10). Thus, he who has the testimony of Jesus also has the spirit of prophecy. And he who through the Holy Spirit testifies of Jesus, experiences that this same spirit proclaims that Jesus Christ did come, that He was crucified for our sins, that He died, that He arose on the third day, that He ascended into heaven, and He [the Holy Spirit] also testifies

to us that Jesus is coming again (compare
John 16:13-14, Revelation 22:17).

## In What Year Will The Redemption Of Israel Take Place?

Some people ask this question, but the form
of this question is not quite correct. Israel's
redemption will not happen in one year, because it already began at the founding of the
state on May 14th, 1948, and continues with
further events and will climax when Jesus
comes. This redemption is not only as the
Bible says, *"an everlasting salvation"* (Isaiah
45:17), but *it is also a multiple one* as Psalms
130:7 says, *"Let Israel hope in the Lord: for
with the Lord there is mercy, and with Him is
plenteous redemption."*

What happened back in 1948 was a tremendous part of the redemption of Israel. At
that time, when the state was founded, we felt
as if the air was vibrating and the Lord was
ready to come at any moment.

Many do not take notice, or have already
forgotten, about this tremendously important event in God's plan of salvation, but it is
still valid today. Something tremendous did
happen! Israel finally came back from their
dispersion, from the concentration camps of

Auschwitz, Treblinda, ... etc. They came into their Promised Land. She actually rose from the grave (compare Ezekiel 37:12,13), she became a nation! The prophet Isaiah saw the founding of the state of Israel in 1948, over 2,700 years ago when he prophesied, *"Who hath heard such a thing? Who hath seen such things? Shall the earth be made to bring forth in one day? or shall a nation be born at once?"* (Isaiah 66:8). And in just two more verses further on, he prophesied about the fulfillment that happened on June 7th, 1967, when Israel liberated Jerusalem during the 6-Day War! For the first time in many thousands of years, Jerusalem became the Capital city of Israel. Verse 10 says, *"Rejoice ye with Jerusalem, and be glad with her, all ye that love her: rejoice for joy with her, all ye that mourn for her."*

## Israel's Redemption Means Judgment Over The Nations

Much has happened since the founding of the state of Israel in 1948, and the liberation of Jerusalem in 1967, in regard to Israel's redemption. One thing, however, which is overlooked too often, is the fact that during this progressive redemption of Israel, and

until the coming of the Messiah, the judgments of the nations are increasing and
running parallel based on the redemption of
Israel. In this regard, we have a very clear
Biblical statement in Isaiah 63:4 where the
Lord speaks, *"For the day of vengeance is in
mine heart, and the year of my redeemed is
come."* Thus, we clearly see that the redemption of Israel, and the judgment over the
nations, runs parallel. This is also expressed
in Isaiah 13:9-11, *"Behold, the day of the Lord
cometh, cruel both with wrath and fierce anger,
to lay the land desolate: and he shall destroy
the sinners thereof out of it. For the stars of
heaven and the constellations thereof shall not
give their light: the sun shall be darkened in his
going forth, and the moon shall not cause her
light to shine. And I will punish the world for
their evil, and the wicked for their inequity;
and I will cause the arrogancy of the proud to
cease, and will lay low the haughtiness of the
terrible."* The reason for this action of God is
found in Isaiah 14:1, *"For the Lord will have
mercy on Jacob, and will yet choose Israel, and
set them in their own land: and the strangers
shall be joined with them."*

Moreover, chapter 13 of Isaiah is very
acute and topical of today. Even if we try to

avoid the interpretation of prophecy for a certain time period, we cannot help but see it clearly pointing to our time. If we are too careful and close our eyes to these signs, we will certainly commit a sin. After Isaiah 13:11, where judgment is pronounced upon the earth, we read in verse 17, *"Behold, I will stir up the Medes against them, which shall not regard silver; and as for gold, they shall not delight in it."* Who are the Medes? They are the people who have mixed with the Persians. We can call these people Medo-Persians (Daniel 2:39; 7:5; 8:20). And today, this Medo-Persian King Khomeini is certainly described fittingly in verse 17, because he is not interested in the economy of Iran. He is not interested in silver or gold, nor does he care much about the many millions of dollars the oil could bring in. The only thing he is concerned with is so clearly expressed through his action, mainly hate and destruction.

We are living in a time today when we are placed in the position of visibly observing the fulfillment of Biblical prophecies before our eyes. The prophet Isaiah confirms this fact in chapter 34, verse 8, *"For it is the day of the Lord's vengeance, and the year of recompenses*

Soviet's invasion army swiftly occupy Kabul.

Western countries are still being blackmailed by barrels of oil.

**Russian Minister of Defense, Dmitir Ustinov, and party chief, Breschznev at a parade of the Soviet military forces on the Red Square in Moscow in November of 1979.**

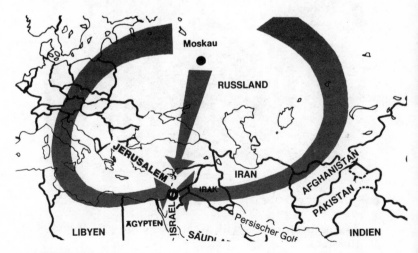

With the help of friendly Soviet countries, Russia is encircling Israel.

The new Soviet-instituted President of Afghanistan, Kar Mal.

Afghanistan rebels with weapons conquered from the Russians.

Russian tanks on the streets in the city of Kabul.

**Russian Navy in the Persian Gulf. The Soviets desire to permanently station themselves in the Middle East is increasing.**

When will the Russian bear put his claws into Iran?

Henry Kissinger and Breschznev with foreign minister Gromeko.

**President Carter's grain embargo to the U.S.A. — Two ships are shown here receiving U.S. grain bound for Russia.**

*for the controversy of Zion."* Yes, indeed, the Lord is concerned about Zion! And what is the world-political opinion about Zionism? The United Nations Assembly in October of 1979, condemned Zionism as a form of Racism by 111 votes, with 11 against, and 14 abstentions. This is the second time since 1977. How then can we possibly be surprised when we witness the nations going downhill?! This in turn means that the judgment over the nation is the year of the judgment of God and corresponds exactly with the controversy of Zion. In this regard, it is very important to observe that the predicted day of vengeance is already beginning. Here are some voices of the press:

## Greatest Danger Ever On World Peace!

"Signs in the Middle East indicate extreme danger! According to Western diplomats, another revolution or war will break out not later than spring of 1980. Secretary General Kurt Waldheim is very worried. He stated that, 'this is the greatest danger to World Peace since the missile crisis in Cuba!' Even if this is avoided, the next crisis will follow for sure nevertheless! Many Islamic countries are working feverishly on their first nuclear bomb."

Peter Scholl-Latour, a prominent T.V. newscaster, stated the following after his Middle East visit:

"At this very hour, Europeans and Americans are still being blackmailed with OIL. In the very near future, several Islamic states will have their own nuclear bombs. In Pakistan, Iraq, and Libya, they are publicly declaring that they are working on a nuclear bomb and one does not need much imagination to know what a man like Ghaddox will do being in the possession of such a destructive weapon.

Without really being aware of it, the Western world is sliding back into the same situation where Europe was during the time of their Crusaders against the Sarazene, the Turks against Islam. But, the Europeans and Americans of today, are far away from the crusader spirit which could certainly be recommended in view of the mystic Islamic military revolutions."

Any type of military action in the Middle East would mean that Western Europe would be without 60% of its energy needs for a period of possibly one half a year. This in turn, means that the flow of energy is not only a question of price, but also a question of availability. It is obvious and clear that it is impossible to reconstruct, in a reasonably short period, an oil field which has been destroyed by bombs. Stockpiles of oil reservoirs are not sufficient enough to last for several months. Experts are predicting the real oil shock will happen in the second half of 1980.

**Fear Of The Third World War Is Growing**

A poll in France shows that 63% of its population believes that the oil crisis will plunge the world into catastrophe. In the spring of 1979, the same poll was conducted in Switzerland, with the result that 48% of the people believed in this coming catastrophe, and in the beginning of 1980, the percentage increased to 64%.

France and other nations have caused judgment upon themselves by their position towards Israel. During the long hostage situation in Tehran, even the anger of President Carter was kindled against the French government, and especially the President:

"Washington now accuses Paris of harboring the irresponsible Khomeini in France for several years and in doing so, has supported this madman. A report by the C.I.A. concludes that the support of Khomeini by France, helped the destruction of the Shah. It also concludes that Paris with its present policies, is supporting Libyan Chief of State Chadaffi. France is trying to guarantee its oil supply through such actions.

Carter has planned, according to observers in Washington, to let France feel the backfire of their actions at the next opportunity."

This worldwide situation of fear, explosion, and judgment was already prophesied thousands of years ago through the events with Israel and Egypt. When Moses was to announce the fourth plague to Pharaoh, he did it under the order of the Lord when he said, *"I will put a division in* (a redemption) *between my people and thy people."* Until that very time, Israel and Egypt were both put under the judgment of God, but at the fifth plague, Israel and Egypt were separated. God's judgment from then on was directed against Egypt only, and judgment was passed over the land of Goshen, where Israel was dwelling. The final redemption of Israel from the power of Egypt at that time, meant the total collapse of the world power, Egypt. Prophetically, we can view Egypt against Israel as the entire world of enemies. This pattern is found as a line going through the entire history until this very day. Take the

collapse of Nazi Germany, which persecuted
Israel to the most bitter extent, but out of it
the state of Israel arose. Today, we are in the
exact same situation, but this time, and for
the first time, it is worldwide.

On one hand, we see the collapse of the
entire Western defense pack under the fear
and weakness of the East. On the other hand,
an unprecedented explosion is standing at
the door in the Middle East, but this time it
will not be aimed at Israel, it will be aimed at
the Western world. The following report
makes this clear to us:

"The entire Free World was shocked when it
heard from the mouth of its defense ministers,
that it will take at least three more years until
NATO forces have modernized their nuclear
capability so it will be able to actually use it.
There are very few people left who believe that
Moscow will let 1980, 1981, or 1982 go by without
taking advantage of this unique hour. Every
single week, one new SS-20 missile is added to the
150 already in existence facing the West. It is
possible that one day the responsible people of the
NATO forces will be required to give account as
to why they let precious years go by without
action. The matter of truth is that the West has
nothing in its hand to effectively oppose a Russian
invasion in Europe."

These new, developing crisis in Europe run parallel with the climaxing crisis in the Middle East where the Soviet Union is openly active in an invasion process. We now see that Russia will invade Israel, and that Afghanistan and Iran no longer belong to the interest of Russia exclusively. In the last few months especially, this "arena" has become highly interesting and topical for the superpower, U.S.A.


## Afghanistan—Iran—Israel

In spite of the fact that the *Frankfurter Allgemeine* writes:

"Prague and Budapest were quickly forgotten, even quicker than the Russians had expected. This will also happen with Afghanistan."

We know, on the grounds of Biblical prophecy, that such a statement is a grave mistake, because Russia is preparing with satellites for the invasion of the Persian Gulf and Israel. Another newspaper report sheds some light on this:

"The armed forces of the D.D.R. (German Democratic Republic) are in constant alert. Holidays and leaves of absence are tightly regulated in such a way that at least 70% of the

armed forces are present at all times. An
additional 15% of its armed forces are ready for
action within 30 minutes. The alarm for preparation practices are sounded at least twice weekly.
After each sound of alarm, troops are expected to
be ready in full-battle gear no less than fifteen
minutes later. The Air Force is ready for action in
less than twenty minutes. Many additional signs
conclude that the troops of the National People's
Army of East Germany are preparing for a
surprise attack."

When we realize for a moment that the
powerless Western World is drifting in a
hopeless direction, fatal to its survival, and at
the same speed Israel's redemption is coming
closer, then we are convinced that no better
times can be expected for the Western world.
Let me repeat, Israel's approaching redemption is an absolute sign of the approaching
destruction of the Western power. If we are to
expect better times economically or politically, then we would have to first erase Israel
from the map.

There are some cool-headed, clear thinking
people who wrote in the *Neue Rheinzeitung:*

"Moscow is taking full advantage of the
seemingly weakness of the United States. Its
next, or second next goal will be Iran."

The very fact that Israel is approaching its

redemption step by step, forces irrevocable judgment upon the world of nations. Many politicians see and sense that an inevitable catastrophe is approaching because of Israel. And this is due to the fact that the "Christian countries" have persecuted and murdered the Jewish people throughout the centuries.

No one would have been surprised about Russia's invasion of Afghanistan, if they would have carefully studied a Middle East map. Russia is simply approaching Israel, and in that way the Word of the Lord is being fulfilled, one step after another. Former Secretary of Energy, James Schlesinger described the Middle East conflict as a "tornado in world politics which is moving today in new, dangerous, and unprecedented ways." To this, Thomas Kielinger writes the following:

"While America is powerlessly watching the fate of the 50 hostages in its Embassy in Tehran, her opposition, the Soviet Union, is marching unhinderingly into the neighbor country of Iran — Afghanistan, to permanently secure its position and influence in that area. This offensive invasion puts everything into the shadow of Moscow's previous military intervention, such as in Eastern Europe after World War II."

This is Biblical fulfillment of prophecy and it is developing quickly in tremendous proportions. Here is an article by the *Daily Telegram:*

"Western nations are no longer concerned about OPEC doubling the oil prices every few months, but the West is now worried about the possibility of getting no oil at all should Russia close the Persian Gulf. Thus, the third World War would simply be won by turning off the tab on the oil faucet."

We may well ask, "Is the Soviet Union really powerful enough to attack and invade Iran?" At the time of this writing, the strength of the Soviet armed forces consists of the following: 3.7 million trained troops, a 1.82 million strong active army, 50 tank divisions, 115 motorized infantry divisions, 8 airborne divisions, and 6 independent airborne brigades. The number of tanks have risen in the last few months to 52,000. Added to this is another 56,000 combat vehicles with the capability of carrying personnel and weapons of different calibers. Over 21,000 pieces of heavy, to medium, to long-range cannons, are at the disposal of this army. To this, Henry Kissinger made the following remark: "A superior military power has always used its power to the political advantage throughout the entire history."

All of these events are developing exactly and precisely according to the prophetic Word, and to such an extent, that even the world press of today is recognizing it very clearly. The Lord proclaims this through the mouth of the prophet Isaiah. *"I the Lord will hasten it in his time"* (Isaiah 60:22).

## America's Chronic Dilemma: The Russian's Winning In The Persian Gulf

To this, *Die Welt* writes the following:

"With the Red Army on Afghanistan soil, a new strategic element has been pushed up front, visible to the political caucus of Washington and revealing its utmost danger. The situation in Iran could change overnight into a new revolution and create a pretext for Russia to intervene militarily. The Russians on the Persian Gulf would thus not be a dream any longer.

This new perspective is tying the hands of America more than anything else in any attempt to free the hostages. Washington is forced to be an observer of the entire Middle East area; any military operation would remain threatening empty words.

Friend and foe have recognized this. Basically,

Carter was and is paralyzed by the overwhelming risk of using force to free the hostages. This could plunge Iran into a situation which would make it necessary to call upon Moscow for help — knowing that the Soviets are very prompt when it comes to answering militarily.

What would be the reaction of the overly criticizing West if America, after using its military strength, would open the road for the Russians in the Gulf?

The present condition is ironic because the danger cannot be avoided by a passive or active course of Washington. Today, the door is open more than ever for a possible Russian invasion.

Even the strongest critics of Carter must confess that a decisive military action would have been possible only the first week after the hostages were taken. In these first days, the surprise of the terrorist's act of taking hostages could have been countered with another surprise action which could possibly have resulted in the freedom of the hostages.

The Afghanistan crisis has given the President a new, legitimate reason to be extremely careful in the matter of Tehran. Even Carter's opponents are not so sure anymore if superior power could solve the problem in Iran, although, they easily point out to the President that he is becoming a casualty of his own weak foreign politics.

The student terrorist groups, which are

occupying the American Embassy, have used this time period to organize themselves into a solid power. Experts recognize in these forms a typical anti-imperialistic formation which previously was observed before communist power exchanges took place in the past.

Even the seemingly undisciplined revolutionary organization outside of the American Embassy has proven to be well-organized. When, on January 1, 1980, the Soviet Embassy was threatened to be stormed by demonstrators, it only took a few minutes to bring three bus loads of military personnel right to the place where they were needed for protection.

A dark cloud of uncertainty is covering Washington. It could lead to the following:

Economic sanction against Iran is without success. Pressure on the White House for some kind of action cannot be postponed any longer. A naval blockade is ordered. Bombing of non-civil installations has begun. Iran declares this action a national emergency. It is standing under the threat of war. This is the exact condition which would permit Russia to intervene militarily according to a 1921 treaty with Iran. This treaty from 1921 was cancelled by Khomeini in October of 1979, but it was declared valid and intact by Russia.

From the power center of the new disciplined anti-imperialistic groups in the American

Embassy in Iran, help is requested from Moscow.
The Red Army would respond immediately and
could be on Iranian soil in a very short time.

This new 'security' element would, of course,
release the American hostages and would immediately exercise its experience in creating 'law
and order Russian style.' The overly-worried
Arabian states (Saudia Arabia and others) would
be assured of territorial integrity and absolute
security! (This dream is only one step away from
reality.)

It was Czar Peter the Great, who urged his
followers to move on from Constantinople to
India, "whoever rules that area would be the
sovereign ruler of the world," he stated.

The southern border of Afghanistan and the
street of Hornus, the energy shipping route of the
free world, are separated by only 500 kilometers.
It could be that 50 American hostages involun-
tarily contributed to the fact that this distance
will soon be closed by Moscow."

From this point of view, the prophetic
Word becomes crystal clear, except that the
news media does not see the rest of it, namely
Isaiah 34:8, *"For it is the day of the Lord's
vengeance, and the year of recompenses for the
controversy of Zion."* This simply means that
all these terrible dangers which are
approaching us today, such as the third

World War, OIL crisis, economic crisis, inflation, moral degeneration, general collapse of peace, etc., have one simple reason; namely God's judgment over the world of nations for Zion's sake. This is not because God's people are being persecuted and rejected, but because the world is rejecting and mocking Him, who on the Cross of Calvary outside Jerusalem, carried away the sins of the world!

## The Number Five

We know that "5" is the number of Grace. As we have already mentioned, Israel was included in the first four plagues in Egypt. There was no difference between Egypt and Israel. Then came the next part, six further terrible judgments came over Egypt. But please note, not over Israel anymore. I repeat, this change is actually happening today. The fact that the children of Israel have come back to the land of their fathers tells us clearly that they are excluded, but they will be protected from the judgment which is breaking forth upon the nations. This fact is very impressively illustrated before our eyes in Joel 3:14-16, *"Multitudes, multitudes in the valley of decision: for the day of the Lord is*

*near in the valley of decision. The sun and the*
*moon shall be darkened, and the stars shall*
*withdraw their shining. The Lord also shall*
*roar out of Zion, and utter his voice from*
*Jerusalem; and the heavens and the earth shall*
*shake: but the Lord will be the hope of his*
*people, and the strength of the children of*
*Israel."*

## Dreams May Not Be "Dreams"

We do not believe that Israel's total redemption will be completed this year, but the events which will precede this complete redemption, as we have already dealt with in this book, are developing with increasing speed. Right now, the Russian Bear has only taken Afghanistan, but very soon he will put his paw into Iran also. And what will happen next? The following notice appeared on December 27th, 1979 in the *Tages Anzeiger:*

"Three well-known Israeli rabbis recently had the same dream simultaneously, which is identical with Ezekiel 38 and 39 (which describes the destruction of Russia with its satellite countries in Israel). According to these dreamers, God will lead His people in battle against Gog, who in the latter days will come to help the king of the north Magog, with the intention of destroying Israel.

This battle will be a preceding sign of the beginning Messianic area of the world. This report of the Apocalyptic dream of those three rabbis hit like a bomb in the religious circle in Israel! Gog is none other than the Soviet Union, which is and will be, supported by Khomeini and other Islamic countries. The three rabbis were named Israel Abu Chatzira, Jekutiel Juda Halberstamm, and Mordechai Sharabi."

We, in general, don't think very much of dreams. Does the Lord not say through the Prophet Jeremiah, *"The prophet that hath a dream, let him tell a dream; and he that hath my word, let him speak my word faithfully. What is the chaff to the wheat? saith the Lord"* (Jeremiah 23:28). However, with this dream we are concerned with three rabbis, three elders of Israel. This concern is the fulfillment of Joel 2:28, which is expressively promised to Israel. *"It shall come to pass afterward, that I will pour out my spirit upon all flesh,"* (that was the first fulfillment on the day of Pentecost in Acts 2) *"and your sons and your daughters shall prophesy, your old men shall dream dreams."* From this point of view, we see the dream of these three old Israelis about the approaching Apocalyptic events in a different light.

**Khomeini, a demonically appearing forerunner of the Antichrist.**

What comes after the old men dream dreams? It is written in Joel 2:30-31, *"And I will show wonders in the heavens and in the earth, blood, and fire, and pillars of smoke. The sun shall be turned into darkness, and the moon ito blood, before the great and the terrible day of the Lord come . . .* and Joel 3:11, *"Assemble yourselves, and come, all ye heathen, and gather yourselves together round about: thither cause thy mighty ones to come down, O Lord."* This means, before the seven year period of tribulation begins, a cosmic catastrophe will take place (for more details, read my book titled, *"There Shall Be Signs From 1948-1982.")* Furthermore, we read in Joel 2:32, *"And it shall come to pass, that whosoever shall call on the name of the Lord shall be delivered: for in Mount Zion and in Jerusalem shall be deliverance, as the Lord hath said, and in the remnant whom the Lord shall call."* Again, in this place, too, we recognize the same line: judgment over the nations, but salvation and protection for Israel!

If the dreams of those three elders of Israel has the same spiritual source as the five dreams at Christmas (one to the wise men from the East, and four to Joseph — compare

Matthew 2), then we'll know absolutely that these events are standing directly at the door. Then we will know that the Soviet Union, with its satellite countries, will come over Afghanistan to Iran, because of their need for oil, and then invade Israel. It is still very

**The Pope — could he be the last forerunner of the false prophet?**

noteworthy and already visible today, that the Soviet's march to the Persian Gulf, according to Revelation 9;14, will be related to the loosening of the four angels of war which are bound in the great River Euphrates, for the Euphrates flows into the Persian Gulf. This decisive step is child's play for the Soviet Union. That is the fundamental reason the Gulf states the oil rich, such as Saudi Arabia, United Arab Emirates, Oman, etc., are shaking today.

Syria and Turkey, which lie directly north of Israel are already shakened by inner unrestlessness. One report says the following:

"Aleppo, the second largest city in Syria, threatens with uncontrollable rebellion and uprising against the government. Almost every night there are street battles between Assad opponents and security officers."

The same bad news is heard from Turkey:

"A decisive political change is developing in Turkey. The Soviet invasions of Afghanistan have put the Turkish military on the highest alert. The entire country is being shaken by bloody demonstrations and numerous political assassinations.

The economic conditions are on the brink of ruin. Prices are on the rise and out of control

(100% inflation in 1979). Business is bad, almost all the essentials needed are missing. Daily, the power supply is out for approximately eight hours in Istanbul, and it is almost impossible to buy coffee or gas. Important industrial facilities are in operation only one-third of their capacities. Thousands of people are being dismissed from their jobs every day. Small businesses are going bankrupt because of the unbelievable climbing costs of production. To avoid a civil war and prevent the Turkish Marxist from calling Moscow for help, the military is trying to keep control. The red army in Turkey would mean an end to NATO's southern defense."

Thus, we see everything is being prepared for Russia's last step into Israel, and everything seems to work just right for Russia today. And that is exactly what these three Rabis dreamed about simultaneously!

## Antichrist and False Prophet — Islam and Rome

Militant Islam, which is preparing Moscow's way into Israel against their own wishes, is beginning to lean visibly on Rome. Out of these two power blocs, two important personalities have risen which have moved the world:

**1**. The bloody man Khomeini. *Time* magazine has declared him "man of the year." We wonder if he is the last forerunner of the Antichrist?

**2**. The Roman Pope, John Paul II, who is holding millions captive with his charisma and charm. Could he be the last forerunner of the false prophet?

Islam and Rome must come closer together because the arising Roman World empire with the Antichrist at its head, will first of all be the great peacemaker which must be recognized by Islam, also. It is written in Revelation 13:4 of the false prince of peace, *"who is able to make war with him?"* And at the same time this man must be recognized by Islam as well as by Israel. And he has to come out of Rome, be accepted by the Jews as the Messiah, and be received by the Arabs as the long awaited redeemer.

## Rebuilding The Temple In Jerusalem

The temple in Jerusalem will soon be rebuilt. It is against the Scripture to assume, as an author of a book recently did, that the rebuilding of the Jewish temple is a Utopia. Also, it is totally against clear Biblical statements to assert that today's Dome of the

**The Dome of the Rock on the temple mount in Jerusalem
is not the desolation of abomination.**

Rock is actually the *abomination of desolation*. The author's writings are based on 25 years' experience as a missionary under Moslems. Experiences are always very helpful, but they prove nothing, and they definitely do not prove the fulfillment of Scripture; decisive alone is the Holy Scripture. The Holy Scripture tells us that the Antichrist *"sitteth in the temple of God"* (II Thessalonians 2:4). Furthermore, it states that in Israel the sacrificial service will be reinstituted and will cease, due to the power of the Antichrist in the middle of the seven years according to Daniel 9:27).

## When Will The Antichrist Be Revealed?

The re-established Roman empire will be based on two strong centers; namely the reunited Europe and the oil-rich Islamic states. For that reason, the unity seeking of some with Islam is in full progress today. We have also become witnesses of a very shameful public demonstration; namely, that of Western politicians humbling themselves before the oil sheiks and at the same time withdrawing themselves from Israel.

Parallel to the political development, we see the physical uniting of Christianity with

Islam. The Pope, who in late 1979 visited
Turkey, spoke openly and frankly about the
uniting religious elements of Christianity
and Islam. He challenged Christians and
Moslems to recognize each others spiritual
ties and to develop them.

Indeed, the Antichrist is on its way!
According to the words of the Lord Jesus,
there will be many false Christs and false
prophets (Matthew 24:24) who have the
power of deception, especially over the
younger generation which is fascinated by it.
But, when the Antichrist himself is revealed,
then the economic crisis, energy crisis,
inflation, recession, and the danger of a
nuclear war will immediately be solved. For
he indeed will create *"Ein Volk, ein Reich ein
Fuhrer"* (one people, one empire, one leader),
compare Revelation 13:3-18, 17:12-13. Nazi
Germany was only a miniature model of the
Antichrist's future role, and all people on
earth whose names are not written in the
Book of Life of the Lamb (Revelation 13:8)
will worship this superman. That is how it
also happened in Nazi Germany. I can still
remember very vividly, when I was deported
from Holland to a working camp in
Germany, the unbelievable fanaticism of

Nazism. In spite of the fact that Germany's cities were bombed heavily and much was destroyed in smoke and ashes, they nevertheless, wrote on the walls in great letters, *"Wir glauben on den Sieg, weil wir den Fuhrer haben"* (we believe in victory for we have the Fuhrer).

We must emphasize here that the solving of all the problems are only seemigly and they will be done by the Antichrist, *"who doeth great wonders"* (Revelation 13:12-13). The fact, however, is that at the same time from God's point of view, terrible and awful judgment will break forth on earth as the book of Revelation reveals in the first seven seals, the sounding of the trumpets, and the veils of wrath. We can see this illustrated with Hitler's empire. On the one side there was an unbelievable, tremendous, economical upswing in Germany. Unemployment ceased, standards of living rose and even crime was miraculously abolished, but on the other side we saw the breaking forth of apocalyptic judgments! Thus, especially in the second half of the anti-Christian rein (3½ years) even a nuclear catastrophe will break forth on earth.

We know that Hitler was only a forerunner

of this terrible super-human which the Bible calls *"that man of sin"* (II Thessalonians 2:3), and today he is seen by those who have spiritual eyes, rising on the horizon. Now, when this man, this Antichrist, suddenly desolves the danger of a world-war and solves all the difficult world problems that existed for centuries, then this miraculous and tremendous experience will lead to Israel's false redemption. Because, as soon as the Lord has raptured His saints, His Church, away from the earth, the Antichrist will begin to reveal himself to Israel, in that he will make a seven-year covenant with them (Daniel 9:27 and Isaiah 28:18).

Khomeini, Pope John Paul II, and all the other "greats" will just fade away in comparison with the coming Antichrist. For he will not only be a sort of super-human, nor the head of the re-established Roman world empire, but he will be the world dictator, the world ruler, and he alone will have power over all kindreds, tongues, and nations (Revelation 13:7). What, however, must happen before that?

## The Rapture Of The Church Of Jesus

When we realize that the redemption of Israel has already begun, how very close the redemption of the Church of Jesus must be! Let me ask another question. Have you been born-again through the grace of God? Do you belong to the Church of Jesus? For I say this again with emphasis — our redemption is drawing very nigh! In view of today's overpowering events, we must also ask the very urgent question, could this sudden **Rapture** of the Church of Jesus happen in our lifetime?

Because the Church and Israel are an integrated part in God's plan of salvation, we see that Israel today is being pressured politically and militarily, because of the fact that their redemption is standing at the door. We must not be surprised that we are suffering spiritual tribulation, for our redemption also draweth nigh — it is even closer. All true children of God sense and feel the powerful grip of the enemy in undeniable and increasing temptations and tribulations.

That Israel is feeling the claws of the Soviet Union politically is a fact, but they are also feeling it militarily. Only one glance at a world map tells quite a story. The publication *Die Rheinpfalz* writes the following:

"Afghanistan has created a new and unique position for the Soviets, enabling them to exercise a political scissor action from South Yemen and Afghanistan. The Soviet Union is creating a superior position enabling them to undermine the entire Arabian peninsula."

East of Israel, the Soviet Union has established a strong-hold in Afghanistan and soon Iran will be added to it. On its western border lies Libya, which is enumerated to be one of the helpers of Russia in Ezekiel 38:5. In south Libya, a large Soviet paratrooper force is stationed and the following report is rather enlightening:

"Russia has a gigantic arsenal of weapons stored in Libya which could easily be transferred in a short period of time to South Yemen or to the Persian Gulf. Furthermore, the Soviet Union has at least 12 airborne divisions which are ready for an attack from its Libya base. The giant *Antonow 22* is permanently stationed with these troops for quick transportation."

Because we are witnessing today, with our own eyes, the preparation of the Soviet Union for its invasion of Israel exactly according to the prophetic Word, it is absolutely essential that we ask the question, "will the rapture of the Church of Jesus, that is the return of Jesus for His own, happen during our time?"

## Jesus Christ Is Coming Again Soon!

At the end of the book of Revelation the exalted Lord said, *"I come quickly"* (Revelation 22:20). When did He say that? Almost two thousand years ago. But, remember that one day to the Lord is as a thousand years, and a thousand years as one day (II Peter 3:8). Let me give a parable. If, for instance, I would say to my wife, "I have to go away for some time, I have to go to several plces and I will be staying overnight somewhere, but I will come back as soon as possible." What will happen is that my wife will expect me back the first day after my departure. More explicitly, she will expect me back the second day! Now, are we not at this time, in the second evening of the day since the departure of our Lord? For Him a thousand years is like a day! I would say yes indeed, for the two thousand years since His departure are coming to a close.

Moreover, we have additional and very plain signs of the return of Jesus Christ that point out that it could happen during our lifetime, for His promise, *"I come quickly,"* is directed to our generation. Why? Our generation is seeing that which many generations before us would have liked to have seen, but they have not seen it; namely the fulfillment, the completion of the Word of God.

The Word of God is complete, it is absolutely perfect, in Psalms 33:4 it states, *"For the Word of the Lord is right; and all His works are done in truth."* No one can shake this eternal rock of truth. It would certainly be primitive and foolish if someone would try to bust a rock with a feather in his hand. Just as primitive are the attempts of Bible critics who try to question the truths of the Bible with their theological questions and dialogues. The eternal rock of the Word of God will outlast all of it.

How absolute and perfect it is, for example, when we view the creation. Nine times we read, *"and God said,"* and from the Bible we receive the report, and we see it today with our own eyes that it became, that *"it was so."* It means all Words the Lord God hath spoken will be fulfilled and are fulfilling themselves constantly to this day. The Lord Jesus expresses the perfectness and completeness of the Word of God in John 6:63 with the following statement, *"The Words that I speak unto you, they are spirit, and they are life.'* This same thing God meant when He called out through Isaiah, *"So shall my word be that goeth forth out of my mouth: it shall not return unto me void, but it shall accomplish that which I please, and it shall prosper in the thing whereto I sent it* (Isaiah 55:11). This statement has a wonderful and deep meaning to us. The Lord wants to emphasize with it that His Word are not the words of man, which so often are empty and void. Today, we live in a time of inflation of words; much is spoken but little is kept. But, with the Word of God it is different, His Words are also action! That is another reason why we expect the return of Jesus Christ anytime, because in our generation the Word of God which was pronounced over Israel and the nations are being fulfilled. And to this complete prophetic Word also belongs the climax, namely the perfection of the Word which became flesh, Jesus Christ. Indeed He is coming again!

## This Generation Shall Not Pass

*"Now learn a parable of the fig tree; When his branch is yet tender, and putteth forth leaves, ye know that summer is nigh; So likewise ye, when ye shall see all these things, know that it is near, even at the doors. Verily I say unto you, This generation shall not pass, till*

*all these things be fulfilled"* (Matthew 24:32-34). What does the Lord Jesus mean with the words, *"till all these things be fulfilled"?* To understand this, one does not need to study theology but, simply read the preceding verses in which He warns, *"Behold, I have told you before ... For as the lightning cometh out of the east, and shineth even unto the west; so shall also the coming of the Son of man be . . . Immediately after the tribulation of those days shall the sun be darkened, and the moon shall not give her light, and the stars shall fall from heaven, and the powers of the heavens shall be shaken ..."* (Matthew 24:25, 27, 29). Then the Lord Jesus continues and speaks about *our* generation which is experiencing the fulfillment of this prophecy, namely the fulfillment of verses 32, 33, and 34, *"Now learn a parable of the fig tree; When his branch is yet tender, and putteth forth leaves, ye know that summer is nigh: So likewise ye, when ye shall see all these things, know that it is near, even at the doors. Verily I say unto you, This generation shall not pass, till all these things be fulfilled."*

Scofield in his commentary on Matthew 24:34 thinks that *this generation* could mean that a future generation, which will suffer tribulation, will see these signs and the completion of it, which is the return of the Lord. Scofield was unable to give more details because he had not experienced the founding of the state of Israel at that time.

Another interesting observation I like to quote is from Albert Springer in the article *The Revelation of Jesus Christ.*

"THIS GENERATION is not given unto us to know the day or the hour of the return of Christ. But the Lord has given us some points to observe and we will do well to take notice of them. *'Now learn a parable of the fig tree; When his branch is yet tender, and putteth forth leaves, ye know that summer is nigh . . . Verily I say unto you, This generation shall not pass, till all these things be fulfilled'* (Matthew 24:32, 34).

The fig tree, which is the nation of Israel, has begun to put forth leaves. After two thousand five-hundred years, the Jewish people have their land again, and they are a nation. This is the most decisive and strongest sign of our times. Generally, it is interpreted that Christ's statement 'this generation' was meant to be the generation at the time of Christ. But this expression can also be translated as *'that generation.'* With this, Christ wanted to emphasize that from the beginning of the growing of the fig tree, until His return, it will take one generation and that generation shall not pass away until all be fulfilled. How long is a Biblical generation?, is our question. According to Matthew 1:17, fourteen generations from the Babylonian captivity until Christ would equal about forty years for one generation. The children of Israel wandered for forty years in the desert. The kingdom of Saul, David, and Solomon lasted forty years each. Furthermore, from the death of Jesus Christ until the destruction of Jerusalem, forty years passed. Therefore, we believe that a Biblical generation is forty years.

It is, therefore, our opinion that we must count from the founding of the state of Israel in 1948, until the coming of Christ, one Biblical generation — forty years. This would bring us to the year 1988. But, please, this date should only be as a guideline, for it is just as dangerous to name the exact year of christ's return as it is to attempt to describe exactly the return itself.

A generation is forty years, and since the founding of the state of Israel in 1948, this generation is coming to an end. The Lord Jesus emphasizes this in Luke 18:31, *'all things that are written by the prophets concerning the Son of man shall be accomplished.'* "

There is an alternative to this interpretation of Springer's, which also is very noteworthy. When the Lord Jesus stated *"this generation shall not pass,"* then our thoughts are immediately focused toward Jerusalem.

For the founding of the state of Israel in 1948 was not the only great happening in God's plan of salvation, but much more — the date June 7, 1967 was when Israel received back the heart of Israel — Jerusalem. Jerusalem was liberated and came under the Jewish rule . . . here the temple mount is located. That was an answer to millions of Jewish prayers for thousands of years!

Jerusalem is the city of the great King. The Lord speaks of this city through the mouth of the prophets, *"Sing and rejoice, O daughter of Zion: for, lo, I come, and I will dwell in the midst of thee . . . And the Lord shall inherit Judah his portion in the holy land, and shall choose Jerusalem again"* (Zechariah 2:10,12). This city alone is the center of world-history and of God's plan of salvation. Whoever had conquered Jerusalem in the past was the ruler of the world. Jerusalem has a great future; the prophets Isaiah and Micah spoke with moving words that the Lord's Law will go out from Jerusalem, and only from Jerusalem will the command be issued for the world to disarm and the nations will come to Jerusalem to learn the law (Compare Isaiah 2 and Micah 4). In this very city, Jerusalem, the cross from Calvary stood, and the greatest

**The view on the mount of Olives "And his feet shall stand in that day upon the mount of Olives, which is before Jerusalem on the east" (Zechariah 14:4).**

event in history happened there: God was in Christ, reconciling the world unto himself (II Corinthians 5:19).

The Lord Jesus Himself describes for us in Luke 21:24 that the return of Jerusalem to Israel as the absolute change in world history for all Gentile nations; *"Jerusalem shall be trodden down of the Gentiles, until the times of the Gentiles be fulfilled."* When Jerusalem was returned to Israel on June 7, 1967, it was the exact beginning of the end of the times for the nations. According to my personal opinion, this is the beginning of *that generation* of which Jesus speaks of in Matthew 24:34. But, we must keep in mind, and carefully think about what the Lord said. One thing He did not say; namely, "this generation shall pass away until all these things be fulfilled," but He did say, *"this generation shall **not** pass until all these things be fulfilled."* This means in practical terms that within these forty years, this Biblical generation, all these things must be fulfilled. With this fact we come to the following conclusions:

**1.** The Rapture can happen at any moment, for we do not know how long the Antichrist has to fully reveal himself after the Rapture.

**2.** The Rapture must take place very soon, for we do not know how many years the Lord has decided to use of this Biblical generation (forty years).

Today we are looking back to the great change in the history of salvation, namely the return of Jerusalem to Israel on June 7, 1967, and we cannot avoid coming to the conclusion that the Lord Jesus meant that this generation which began in 1967 will not pass until all of it has come to pass.

What tremendous times we are living in! Yet, in all our interpretations, we must not lose sight of the statement in the Scripture, *"For we know in part"* (I Corinthians 13:9). Thus, it is important that one must never come to the conclusion that what he knows right now is the only correct interpretation. Rather, as we walk in His light, we should increasingly receive knowledge upon knowledge, and light upon light. And the more we approach the returning of Jesus, the more the Lord enlightens our spirit through His Holy Spirit, and the less we are permitted to avoid the consequences of the plain statement of our Lord Jesus Christ in Matthew 24:34 *"Verily I say unto you, This generation shall not pass, till all these things be fulfilled."* With this, the admonition of the apostle Peter becomes very topical for us, *"We have also a more sure word of prophecy; whereunto ye do well that ye take heed, as unto a light that shineth in a dark place, until the day dawn, and the day star arise in your hearts"* (II Peter 1:19).

## Fulfilled In Smallest Details

Another vital reason we can expect the return of the Lord Jesus very soon, is because the fulfilling of the prophetic Word is becoming visible in the smallest detail. We have mentioned several details in this book already.

At the end of the creation report we read in Genesis 2:1, *"Thus the heavens and the earth were finished, and all the host of them."* These words include all the finest details; the trees with their leaves, all the living creatures with their peculiarities, the invisible bacteria, etc. Nothing was missing! God always fulfills and completes His Word!

Later when God the Lord had fulfilled the promises He made to Jacob and his descendants, and they possessed the land of promise and lived in it, we read in Joshua 21:45, *"There failed not ought of any good thing which the Lord had spoken unto the house of Israel; all came to pass."*

This fact is also repeating itself quickly today. Everything we have dealt with in this book, thus far, is the fulfillment of prophecy thousands of years old. A press report clearly shows how the entire world is involved when it comes to the Middle East. Carter, for

Desperation and hopelessness has marked the faces of those who attempt to resist the Soviet invasion.

Refugees from Afghanistan are flooding into neighboring Pakistan.

instance, quickly lifted an arms embargo against Pakistan after the quick and successful Afghanistan invasion by Soviet Russia.

"Pakistan, after accepting more than 600,000 Afghanistan refugees has suddenly come into the firing line of the Soviet activity, and Iran is beginning to feel it, too. All of a sudden they are threatened from another side they did not expect. Most countries, including other Arab states, such as Saudi Arabia, Egypt, and also Turkey, have strongly condemned the Soviet invasion of Afghanistan. The Peoples Republic of China prove to be very nervous and agitated as they increase their troop strength in Sinkiang close to the border of Pakistan."

This is the accelerated fulfillment of God's Word as proclaimed by His prophets. But, we have another urgent reason to believe that the Lord is coming very soon to take His blood-bought ones into the house of the heavenly Father, unto Himself, because . . .

## Eternity Breaks Into Time!

It is not only a figure of speech when people say "time is just flying by!" Indeed, time is actually flying by very quickly. Why is this? This phenomenon of increased speed of time has some explanations. Some explain that this is due to the fact that we are moving faster than in earlier times. Others explain that it is due to our modern communication's capability. Man has to observe and digest so many new things today, but, these things are only the result of the fact that prophecy is being fulfilled by a large part, and therefore, time is running out quickly.

Let's take, as an example, an hour glass. The sand runs from the top bowl to the bottom one. At the beginning, only a little sand is in the bottom part, and one just knows there is some time left. But, as soon as half of the sand has run into the bottom part, less sand begins to be seen in the upper part, which means less time, until only a very tiny bit is left, and this sand just seems to rush through and suddenly the time is up! Then the time allotted for a purpose has run out, and it will never return.

When the Bible calls to each one of us, as the angels of God once did to Lot, *"make haste, save your soul,"* it has a definite purpose. Maybe this moment could be your last. It is not a coincidence that you are reading this book, for the Spirit of God wants to move you away from your indifference. He wants to wake you up out of your spiritual sleep. Right now He is calling to you, *"make haste, save your soul!"*

The constant decrease in time, which we have at our disposal is even pressed upon by the approaching eternity. For that very reason, worldwide events are toppling over each other. Regarding Israel, we recognize that our time is soon up. Israel is God's time piece on earth and through it, eternity is breaking into time, Jesus is coming soon!

Since the appearance of Israel on the horizon, and in spite of this irrevocable fact that the Rapture of the Church of Jesus can happen at any time, there are many children of God who dare to keep their bank account open, to increase their capital, their savings, and to continue to draw interest upon interest. Has not the Lord Jesus warned us clearly and emphatically in Matthew 6:19, *"Lay not up for yourselves treasures upon earth, where moth and rust doth corrupt, and where thieves break through and steal: But lay up for yourselves treasures in heaven."* What will happen with all your savings, with all your property and goods, if the Rapture would take place today? These valuables and properties, which could have been invested in the work for Jesus Christ, will now be turned over into the hands of the Antichrist. Therefore, think

**Do you belong to the foolish or wise virgins?**

about it today, and work with all the means that you have at your disposal which the Lord has entrusted to you. Do as your Lord did, *"I must work the works of him that sent me, while it is day: the night cometh, when no man can work"* (John 9:4)!

## The Number 7

There is also a mathematical reason why we can expect the Lord very soon. Our Lord did say, *"But of that day and hour knoweth no man, no, not the angels of heaven, but my Father only"* (Matthew 24:36), but strangely enough the Lord Jesus does not mention the *year*. For that reason Daniel searched out the years.

The number of fullness, the number of God, is seven. We are standing before the beginning of the seventh Millenium. In the year 1897 the first Zionist Congress took place in Basel, Switzerland under the guidance of Theodor Herzl. Fundamentally speaking, that was the time when the state of Israel was re-born, because Theodor Herzl during that Congress proclaimed prophetically the words "whether or not you want to believe it, and this is not fiction, I today, have founded the state of Israel!" Thus, we could say the state of Israel was founded in Switzerland. Purposely, I believe that is the reason for the mysterious blessing which lies on this tiny little country, it was even spared of both world wars. Did not the Lord promise to Abraham the first Israelite *"I will bless them that bless thee"* (Genesis 12:3).

What occurred *seventy* years after the first Zionist Congrss of 1897 (when Israel spent 70 years in Babylonian captivity)? Answer, Israel received Jerusalem back, and this happened exactly on June 7, 1967. Ten years later, in 1977, Professor Bloch stated during our Prophetic Congress in Jerusalem that "we are now experiencing a political turnabout in Israel." This resulted not only because a Bible-believing government came to power, but because in November of 1977, the Egyptian President, Anwar Sadat came to visit Jerusalem for the first time. [For more details, read my book *Begin With Sadat*].

These are just a few numbers of the years which clearly tell us how late it is on the world clock!

## What If The Lord Came In One Hour?

Besides the visible outward signs, there are also inner warning signals which tell us that the coming of the Lord Jesus is in preparation, because the Holy Spirit urges the members of the Church of Jesus, increasingly, to prepare for the meeting with their Lord, to be absolutely ready for His sudden appearance. It is the same Spirit which shouts through the prophet Amos, the prophet of the Old Covenant, to the people, *"prepare to meet thy God, O Israel"* (Amos 4:12).

Today, there are children of God across the face of the earth who under the guidance and conviction of the Holy Spirit, have the courage to think about the sudden coming of the Lord Jesus at the Rapture. Unfortunately, in affluent (rich) countries there are very few who are actually waiting and preparing for the coming of the Lord, because the riches and the luxury of the world is suffocating the seed of the Word of God in most of those believers.

Let us, at this very moment, think to the end, think about the sudden appearance of the Lord Jesus. If the Lord were to come in one hour, what would you have to do to make

everything right in this one hour? Don't
refuse to enumerate everything — leave
nothing out — think to the end! Never before
did the Lord so impressively put before our
eyes the words of Hebrews 12:14, *"Follow
peace with all men, and holiness, without
which no man shall see the Lord."* These inner
questions of: Do I live in peace with all men?
Is there any grudge I carry against anyone in
my heart? Do I live in sanctification? Am I
really ready if the Lord would come right
now? These questions are asked by the Holy
Spirit to believers around the world today,
because *"the Spirit and the bride say, Come . . .
Amen. Even so, come, Lord Jesus!"* (Revelation 22:17, 20).

I repeat — the Lord can appear any minute
for the Rapture. For that reason, I must ask
you a very burning and topical question. Are
you filled with the oil of the Holy Spirit? Are
you, in reality, prepared for Him? Or, will it
be, that in that very hour, when all of a
sudden He comes, you will be shocked and
you will weep and shout and cry after those
who have been raptured, *"Give us of your oil;
for our lamps are gone out"* (Matthew 25:8).

Oh, my dear friends, I have been shocked
and shaken at the thought of how terrible it

must be for many Christians who count themselves to the Church of Jesus, but never have taken sanctification seriously and are like these foolish virgins, who, when approaching the night of the end of time, will cry out, *"no light,"* *"no oil!"* And, they will shout and plead with the Lord: *"Lord, Lord open to us!"* But, from inside the very shocking and irrevocable answer will be heard, *"Verily I say unto you, I know you not"* (Matthew 25:12).

## Today's Three-Fold Happening:

**1.** Darkness is breaking forth upon the world with terrorism, anarchism, wars, rumors of wars, and crisis upon crisis as never before.

**2.** In the hearts of many believers the light is being newly aflamed, especially in the children of God who walk in holiness and sanctification. They love Jesus and have surrendered everything to Him unto the alter. They are redeemed and liberated from everything of the world; they are those who can say with all their hearts, *"yes, Lord Jesus, come!"*

**3.** For many believers the lights are going out today. They are the ones who have put

*"water into the wine."* They have lost their
first love for the Lord, and to these, the Lord
says, *"Remember therefore from whence thou
art fallen, and repent, and do the first works;
or else I will come unto thee quickly, and will
remove the candlestick out of his place, except
thou repent"* (Revelation 2:5).

If you belong to those named in category 3,
I am asking you, why has it become dark
within you? I could write a book about the
things an evil tongue can do, for, during my
32 years of service for the Lord, I have
experienced much tribulation due to evil
tongues. An evil tongue is able to separate
faithful friends and brethren; it is able to
degrade proven disciples of Jesus; it destroys
the unity of the Spirit (compare James 3). I
am sure there are such among my readers
who have never repented over the sin of an
evil tongue. You have never confessed to the
Lord, in truth, about your greediness, but
now you still can confess and repent — the
Lord is waiting for you!

## Steps On The Way To The Rapture

The Rapture, itself, is a wonderful and
vital event yet to be fulfilled, and it is necessary that we take a closer look into it.

Giglal — here Elijah went up to heaven by a whirlwind.

Because, if the Rapture were to take place after you have read this book, then you will know what is really happening. In I Corinthians 15:51-52 we read, *"Behold, I shew you a mystery; We shall not all sleep, but we shall all be changed, In a moment, in the twinkling of an eye, at the last trump: for the trumpet shall sound, and the dead shall be raised incorruptible, and we shall be changed."* Here the apostle Paul speaks about the Rapture, and

Bethel — here Elijah said, "Tarry, I pray thee, here; for the Lord has sent me to Bethel."

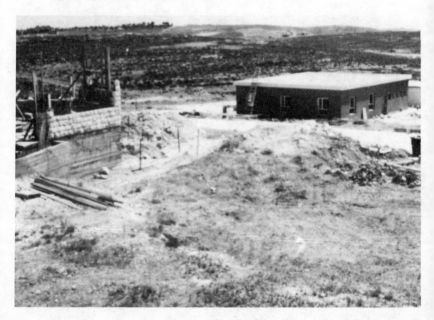

with it, he reveals something peculiar about this event, namely that it is a mystery. Something which has not been revealed is still a mystery to most. Many Christians have no idea or no knowledge about this, because they have so little fear of God in their heart. But, the more you fear God, the more you will understand God's mysteries.

Psalms 25:14 says something very fundamental about God's eternal plan, *"The secret of the Lord is with them that fear him; and he will show them his covenant."* The mystery of the Rapture, that is the sudden taking away of all born-again persons from earth towards heaven, is very topical today, because it is the event that is actually standing at our doorstep. It will happen suddenly because all born-again persons are already one body in the exalted Christ. With our intellect, we cannot conceive the speed and suddenness in which it will take place. but, we do know that the body of Jesus Christ will be revealed in glory, when all members will be Raptured to Him.

This tremendous event is also a mystery because it is proclaimed so little. And yet, it is clearly and plainly written in your Bible. How unfortunate it is that so few believers are, in actual fact, walking and preparing themselves toward that one goal. Philippians 3:20 shows a waiting Christian, *"For our conversation* (walk) *is in heaven; from whence also we look for the Saviour, the Lord Jesus Christ."* This means in practical terms that we are totally free from all earthly things and absolutely ready for departure at any moment. Many are living today as if there is no Rapture to expect at all. Yet, we not only have very clear and direct statements in the Scripture about the Rapture, but we also have prophetic illustrations of the past which point to the coming Rapture. Furthermore, we also have in the Scripture, prophetic pictures pointing to the future, that will happen after the Rapture.

Let us look at some prophetic examples of the past, such as the prophet Elijah and Enoch. Elijah lived during a time of apostacy. He himself stated, *"I, even I only, remain a prophet of the Lord"* (I Kings 18:22). We have to enumerate four different steps we find in the Scripture which led Elijah to his rapture.

*"And it came to pass, when the Lord would take up Elijah into heaven by a whirlwind, that Elijah went with Elisha from Gilgal"*

Jericho — and Elijah said unto him, "Elisha, tarry here, I pray thee; for the Lord has sent me to Jericho."

**(Step 1).** *"And Elijah said unto Elisha, Tarry here, I pray thee; for the Lord hath sent me to Bethel"* **(Step 2).** *"And Elisha said unto him, As the Lord liveth, and as thy soul liveth, I will not leave thee. So they went down to Bethel. And the sons of the prophets that were at Bethel came forth to Elisha, and said unto him, Knowest thou that the Lord will take away thy master from thy head today? And he said, Yea, I know it; hold ye your peace. And*

The Jordan River: Elijah said unto him, "Tarry, I pray thee here; for the Lord has sent me to Jordan."

*Elijah said unto him, Elisha, tarry here, I pray thee; for the Lord hath sent me to Jericho"* **(Step 3).** *"And he said, As the Lord liveth, and as thy soul liveth, I will not leave thee. So they came to Jericho. And the sons of the prophets that were at Jericho came to Elisha, and said unto him, Knowest thou that the Lord will take away thy master from thy head today? And he answered, Yea, I know it; hold ye your peace. And Elijah said unto him, Tarry, I pray thee, here; for the Lord hath sent me to Jordan"* **(Step 4)** . . . *"And it came to pass, as they still* *went on, and talked, that, behold, there appeared a chariot of fire, and horses of fire, and parted them both asunder; and Elijah went up by a whirlwind into heaven"* (II Kings 2:1-11).

## Summarizing, these are the four steps:

**1.** Gilgal (means "rolling off")

2. Bethel (means "house of God")

**3.** Jericho (the first city which was conquered by Israel through faith)

**4.** Jordan (means "descending")

As a second example for the Rapture of the past, is Enoch. About Enoch we read, *"And Enoch lived sixty and five years, and begat Methuselah: And Enoch walked with God after he begat Methuselah three hundred years, and begat sons and daughters. And all the days of Enoch were three hundred sixty and five years. And Enoch walked with God: and he was not; for God took him"* (Genesis 5:21-24). These men went directly to God without going through death. These two were similar to each other in their relationship. They were prophets of judgment. Enoch prophesied, *"Behold, the Lord cometh with ten thousands of his saints, To execute judgment upon all, and to convince all that are ungodly among them of*

"And it came to pass, as they still went on, and talked, that, behold, there appeared a chariot of fire, and horses of fire and parted them both assunder; and Elijah went up by a whirlwind into heaven [II Kings 2:11]."

*all their ungodly deeds which they have ungodly committed, and of all their hard speeches which ungodly sinners have spoken against him"* (Jude 14-15). And Elijah spoke, *"As the Lord God of Israel liveth, before whom I stand, there shall not be dew nor rain these years, but according to my word"* (I King 17:1).

Enoch walked with God and Elijah was standing before God. Both were raptured before the judgment, of which they testified, broke loose. Enoch walked with God until his rapture; for three hundred long years he experienced many things we don't know of. Elijah experienced the four steps we just mentioned.

Examples of the Rapture of the future are the two witnesses of which Revelation II speaks of. According to our knowledge of the Scripture, these two witnesses are identical with Moses and Elijah. After the Antichrist kills them, they will arise and stand up on their feet again. Then they will be raptured to heaven. *"And when they shall have finished their testimony, the beast that ascendeth out of the bottomless pit shall make war against them, and shall overcome them, and kill them. And their dead bodies shall lie in the street of*

*the great city, which spiritually is called
Sodom and Egypt, where also our Lord was
crucified. And they of the people and kindreds
and tongues and nations shall see their dead
bodies three days and a half, and shall not
suffer their dead bodies to be put in graves.
And they that dwell upon the earth shall
rejoice over them, and make merry, and shall
send gifts one to another; because these two
prophets tormented them that dwelt on the
earth. And after three days and a half the
spirit of life from God entered into them, and
they stood upon their feet; and great fear fell
upon them which saw them. And they heard a
great voice from heaven saying unto them,
Come up hither. And they ascended up to
heaven in a cloud; and their enemies beheld
them"* (Revelation 11:7-12).

There is a difference, however, between
our Rapture which is about to happen soon,
and the two witnesses. Our Rapture will not
be witnessed by the world, they will notice it
only because suddenly we will disappear
from the earth. But, the rapture of these two
witnesses will be observed visibly by their
enemies as we have just seen from our text.

Yet, there is a third Rapture the Scripture
speaks about, which will also happen after

our Rapture, the Rapture of the Church. It is totally different from ours. When Jesus Christ comes in great power and glory as King of kings, and when all eyes of the earth will see Him and will weep and lament, the Lord will send His angels with the sound of the trumpet, and gather all the Jews from the entire world and Rapture them to Israel (compare Mark 13:24-27). Thus, we see three steps in His first coming, and also three steps in the second coming of Jesus. At His coming and during His work here on earth it was:

1. His coming, as a child in Bethlehem;

2. His public appearance with the message, *"repent for the Kingdom of heaven is at hand;"*

3. and His re-appearance after His resurrection for forty days on Earth.

The three steps of His second coming which we expect are:

1. For His Church as the Bridegroom to take home His bride (compare I Thessalonians 4:16-17). That is the time the Great Tribulation will start on earth under the rulership of the Antichrist.

2. The Lord is coming again in great power and glory as King of kings with His Church for the nations. This is written in

Matthew 24:29-30. *"Immediately after the tribulation of those days shall the sun be darkened, and the moon shall not give her light, and the stars shall fall from heaven, and the powers of the heavens shall be shaken: And then shall appear the sign of the Son of man in heaven: And then shall all the tribes of the earth mourn, and they shall see the Son of man coming in the clouds of heaven with power and great glory."*

3. The Lord will come as the Messiah and Priest for His people Israel. All the Jews of the world will then be back in Israel. They will have been Raptured, so to speak, back to the land Israel as we have already seen, *"And he shall send his angels with a great sound of a trumpet, and they shall gather together his elect from the four winds, from one end of heaven to the other"* (Matthew 24:31). This *Rapture* will mean at the same time the coming of the Lord for the nations.

At this third step of the coming of Jesus, all of Israel will be ready for conversion, they will be prepared for it, for they will witness how the Lord in great power and glory will come for the nations and make an end of the Antichrist. That will be the time when *"the Veil of Moses"* will be removed from their

The 29'th Zionist Congress in Jerusalem. Inspite of
Israel's hard work and opening of all avenues as shown
here, during the 29th Zionist Congress in Jerusalem, to
move many more Jewish people to immigrate to Israel,
millions are still living in their respected guest countries
around the world. But when the Lord comes with great
power and glory, they will be raptured by his angels to
Israel.

eyes, and they will see the Lamb of God. That
is the Rapture of Israel from among the
nations to the land of Israel. The prophet
Ezekiel also speaks about that in chapter
39:28, *"Then shall they know that I am the
Lord their God, which caused them to be led
into captivity among the heathen: but I have
gathered them unto their own land, and have
left none of them any more there."* There is an
important difference we must note between

the Rapture of the Jews from all the world to the land of Israel, and the Rapture of the Church to heaven to their Lord. The Jews are Raptured to Israel to be converted, but the Church is Raptured to the Lord towards heaven because they had been converted.

In spite of the many examples and illustrations in the Bible about the past and the future of the Rapture, it remains a mystery to many who are concerned about this great event. This is because the Rapture does not concern itself only with those who are born-again, but it concerns itself with the PERSON of Jesus Christ. For that very same reasons, Paul spoke about a three-fold mystery. When he spoke about the person of Jesus Christ, he said, *"to speak the mystery of Christ"* (Colossians 4:3). Concerning His Church, that is His body, he saith, *"This is a great mystery: but I speak concerning Christ and the church"* (Ephesians 5:32). And finally, when he spoke about the Rapture of the Church to the Lord, he saith, *"Behold, I shew you a mystery; We shall not all sleep, but we shall all be changed"* (I Corinthians 15:51).

With the help of the Holy Spirit we will attempt to see these three mysteries — Christ, the Church, and the Rapture — to show that they are united inseparably to each other. But, before we get into it, the following question:

Do you believe that the Lord Jesus, in His glorified body has actually ascended into heaven? What actually was His ascension then? Shortly before He went to Calvary, He said something in this connection, with simple words to His disciples, *"Let not your heart be troubled: ye believe in God, believe also in me. In my Father's house are many mansions: if it were not so, I would have told you. I go to prepare a place for you. And if I go and prepare a place for you, I will come again, and receive you unto myself; that where I am, there ye may be also"* (John 14:1-3). With these words the Lord wants to show you a very great mystery; namely if you are born-again, then you are a living member integrated into the body of Jesus Christ of which He is the head. Ultimately, this means that in spirit, all born-again believers have already been Raptured with the Lord on the day of ascension!

Paul also speaks about this trmendous, already accomplished event, *"And hath raised us up together, and made us sit together in heavenly places in Christ Jesus"*

(Ephesians 2:6). We simply over-read these words too often. But these words mean that you are already in heaven! No matter how you feel or how the condition of your body is, the fact is that you dwell in your sinful flesh, which is deteriorating unto death — and in this perishable tabernacle you are walking the earth! This wonderful organic unity with Jesus Christ is such a glorious reality, that the Rapture must take place as soon as the fullness of the members of the body of Jesus have come in (compare Romans 11:25).

When Jesus Christ dwells in you, and the wonderful mystery is being revealed clearer and clearer, then you begin to see it more and more with your inner eye. Listen to Paul as he talks about this fact in Colossians 1:26 and 27, *"Even the mystery which hath been hid from ages and from generations, but now is made manifest to his saints: To whom God would make known what is the riches of the glory of this mystery among the Gentiles; which is Christ in you, the hope of glory."*

We already saw the four steps of the rapture concerning Elijah. The first one was Gilgal, which means "rolling off." Gilgal was the place where Israel finally came after wandering aimlessly for 40 years in the desert, and here they were circumcised. The Lord said to Joshua, *"This day have I rolled away the reproach of Egypt from off you. Wherefore the name of the place is called Gilgal unto this day"* (Joshua 5:9).

The first step to the Rapture is Jesus Christ in you! Jesus Christ wants to enter and dwell in your heart and He will, but only when you open your heart in child-like faith and ask Him, *"Come into my heart, Lord Jesus!"* Then He rolls away all of the reproach of sin, for He carried our shame, sin, and reproach away on the Cross of Calvary. We read in Hebrews 12:2, *"for the joy that was set before Him endured the cross, despising the shame."* That is what He did, and He wants you to experiene Gilgal!

In Jesus, you suddenly begin to realize, and are totally convinced, that the Rapture will happen and you realize in what dispensation we are living in God's plan of salvation.

A question we must ask is: Will we be raptured during, before or after the Great Tribulation? The Great Tribulation consists of the seven year rulership of the Antichrist. This period is mentioned several times in the Bible; such as in Daniel, or mentioned by the Lord Jesus Himself in Matthew 24:21. The acceptance of the Antichrist will be a logical result of today's condition of the world: powerless, indecisiveness, and turmoil of the nations. No government in the world can execute their task without being hindered or completely stopped by demonstrations, rebellions, strikes, uprisings, etc. And these governments around the world are collectively yearning for one man who is able to take law and order in his hands and execute it. All good and decent citizens who believe in law and order, but have not surrendered to Jesus, will joyfully welcome and accept the Antichrist.

Another thing is clearly stated in the Scripture; namely that the Antichrist cannot unfold himself as long as the Holy Spirit and the Church of Jesus remain on earth. *"And now ye know what withholdeth that he might be revealed in his time. For the mystery of inequity doth already work: only he who now letteth will let, until he be taken out of the way. And then shall that Wicked be revealed, whom the Lord shall consume with the spirit of his mouth, and shall destroy with the brightness of his coming"* (II Thessalonians 2:6-8). This means that the Church of Jesus will definitely be Raptured before the Great

Tribulation!

If Jesus dwells in you as the Hope of Glory, then this inner assurance is a wonderful and triumphant security. Before the Lord Jesus ascended into heaven with His glorified body, He said, *"I will not leave you comfortless: I will come to you"* (John 14:18). And when Jesus ascended into heaven, all His members were already with Him in Spirit, just in the same way as we see with Abraham as we find it so wonderfully written in Hebrews 7:9-10, *"And as I may so say, Levi also, who receiveth tithes, paid tithes in Abraham. For he was yet in the loins of his father, when Melchisedec met him."* Because all believers, who throughout the centuries would still have to be born-again were already in the Lord when He ascended with His glorified body into heaven. Paul speaks of the body of Jesus and of His ascension in one breath, *"Wherefore he saith, When he ascended up on high, he led captivity captive, and gave gifts unto men. (Now that he ascended, what is it but that he also descended first into the lower parts of the earth? He that descended is the same also that ascended up far above all heavens, that he might fill all things.) And he gave some, apostles; and some, prophets; and some, evangelists; and some,*

*pastors and teachers; For the perfecting of the
saints, for the work of the ministry, for the
edifying of the body of Christ: Till we all come
in the unity of the faith, and of the knowledge of
the Son of God, unto a perfect man, unto the
measure of the stature of the fullness of Christ:
That we henceforth be no more children, tossed
to and fro, and carried about with every wind
of doctrine, by the sleight of men, and cunning
craftiness, whereby they lie in wait to deceive;
But speaking the truth in love, may grow up
into him in all things, which is the head, even
Christ: From whom the whole body fitly joined
together and compacted by that which every
joint supplieth, according to the effectual
working in the measure of every part, maketh
increase of the body unto the edifying of itself
in love"* (Ephesians 4:8-16).

Thus, we see that the ascension of Jesus,
His Church, and the Rapture, fundamentally
speaking, are one! The only thing is that there
is a time period between it. For that reason, it
is totally false and misleading to speak about
the Rapture as an event separated from our
position today in Christ. Paul reveals this
very clearly when he speaks to the Thessalonians, *"For if we believe that Jesus died and
rose again, even so them also which sleep in*

*Jesus will God bring with him"* (I Thessalonians 4:14).

We, the Church of Jesus, must also take the same steps that Elijah took towards his rapture. These steps must be accomplished first.

**1.** GILGAL (Rolling Off) — You must leave the shame of the world behind.

**2.** BETHEL (House of God) — Your conversion happened, you are on the way to the Rapture, and the Lord is preparing a dwelling place for you, *"In my father's house are many mansions"* (John 14:2).

**3.** JERICHO — Means that in faith only, not sight, will we claim and keep the victory of Jesus.

The apostle Paul also speaks about these steps. Let us see two examples: *"and so shall we ever be with the Lord"* (I Thessalonians 4:17), that is BETHEL. Of Jericho, he speaks in verse 14, *"For if we believe that Jesus died and rose again."* That means, in other words, in spite of all our tribulation and temptation, we are one with Jesus in His death, and in His resurrection.

From this point of view, we see, believe, and know that the Rapture is standing at the door. Elisha, the successor of Elijah, who represents for us the people of Israel, is already accompanying us on our way to the Rapture. We know that Elisha could not be divided anymore from Elijah. They walked together, but at the Rapture, Elijah went to heaven, and Elisha remained. We too, who are genuine Christians can hardly be separated from Israel, and Israel does not want to be separated from us. We know this from practical experience through the mail and from telephone calls from Israel by highly-placed personalities of Israel. But, as it was in the case of Elisha and Elijah, in the same way, Israel will take over our task and office here on earth. That is already the fourth step to the Rapture, and at this point, many are stuck and refuse to go on further, *"And Elijah said unto him, Tarry, I pray thee, here; for the Lord hath sent me to Jordan. And he said, As the Lord liveth, and as thy soul liveth, I will not leave thee. And they two went on"* (II Kings 2:6). Strangely enough, no one else but Elisha went with him, for we read in verse 7, *"And fifty men of the sons of the prophets went, and stood to view afar off: and they two stood by Jordan."* Just as these 50 men, many today are standing back when it comes to the last step. They refuse to do the essential. The first three steps are done by many: GILGAL, we repeat, is the rolling away of our sins; BEHTEL, is the house of the Lord; and JERICHO, is victory in faith. And then comes the last step, which is JORDAN. It means the surrendering of one's own life! Indeed, not only "Christ died for me" (Romans 5:6), but now "I died for Christ" (Romans 6:5). That is the other side of the cross. The Jordan River has a tremendous significance. After Israel aimlessly wandered in the desert for 40 years, they crossed the Jordan and were circumcised in Gilgal. What an experience! Here the Jordan River parted, and the Israelis went through. They left behind the desert life, the old life. They went through the Jordan and moved into the Promised Land.

Now we see Elijah and Elisha standing in front of the Jordan. Elijah took his coat, hit it on the water and it divided. Both had already denied their own life, and both of them went into the death of Jesus, but not those 50 men, the followers, those religious prophetic students, they did not go! They remained in the position of spectators. They did not go through the Jordan. This testimony is given in a rather short, but powerful sentence: *"and stood to view afar off, and they two stood by Jordan.*" If you refuse to take this last step, then you cannot remain a member of the body of Jesus. This is the very reason the Lord warns us with great seriousness, "*Abide in me, and I in you*" (John 15:4). He was telling us, when I have ascended into heaven, remain in me and I will remain in you. Ephesians 2:6 says in this regard, "*And have raised us up together, and made us sit together in heavenly places in Christ Jesus.*" Thus, it is absolutely essential that we keep up a constant living relationship with the Lord Jesus!

On the grounds of these very serious facts, we cannot believe in an *automatic* Rapture of all believers. The Scripture teaches differently. It is too often over-read in the Scripture, the Lord's proper succession in naming the essentials, *If a man abide not in me, he is cast forth as a branch, and is withered; and men gather them, and cast them into the fire, and they are burned*" (John 15:6). I cannot help but identify those as such who once were converted, and through the rebirth are integrated in the body of Jesus Christ, but begin to live their own lives again and do not remain in Jesus. They are permitting themselves to be moved about by their own lusts and compassions and refuse to hear anything about deeper purification and sanctification. Such, I believe, will have no living relationship with the Lord at the Rapture. The resurrection power of Jesus cannot penetrate them because the Godly connection and the living unity were already interrupted and broken long ago! John warned us about these terrible experiences very emphatically, *"And now, little children, abide in Him; that, when He shall appear, wee may have confidence, and not be ashamed before Him at His coming"* (I John 2:28).

When the Lord comes suddenly, the people will notice that they have missed the Rapture. Why? Because without holiness, no one will see the Lord (Hebrews 12:14).

What will happen to these people who have been converted, of which there are many, but have never become a part of or a member of the body of Jesus. The Bible tells us, *"neither shall any man pluck them out of my hand"* (John 10:28). This means they are not lost, but they will be left at the Rapture and will have to go through the Great Tribulation. With tears and weeping, they will repent over their sins of living for themselves and living with and for the world. The life which they loved so much before the Rapture will now have to be surrendered in order to belong to the *great multitude*, which no one could number in Revelation 7:9. Thus, they have washed their clothes in the Blood of the Lamb, but they will lose the glory of the Church of Jesus. And as mentioned, under the rule of the Antichrist, they will be forced to deny their life (compare Revelation 13:15).

If the Rapture would take place at this very moment, while you are reading this book, will you participate? Or will you be left behind? The Lord Jesus said, *"Then shall two be in the field; the one shall be taken, and the other one left. Two women shall be grinding at the mill; the one shall be taken, and the other left"* (Matthew 24:40, 41). Do you have a living connection with the Lord Jesus, or has your heart grown cold? How about your spirit of prayer, has it been extinguished? Then repent, and come back to Jesus now!

## What Will Be The Results Of A Third World War?

First of all, it will be rather positive for Israel. While we are sending the manuscripts for this book to the printer, and the Soviets have not broken through to the Persian Gulf and towards Israel, it is not necessary to mention that the last aggression, the last invasion of Russia, is at the door. For many years we have repeatedly stated that Ezekiel 38 and 39 will soon be fulfilled. According to chapter 38, verse 8, it will be fulfilled in the *last days*. This time period, the *last days*, are now. First of all, it means the last days for the Church of Jesus on earth.

What, we have to ask, will be the result of a third World War, which basically speaking, has already begun? I repeat, for Israel it will be positive. For the threat from the far North will then be done away with. Then a great military and political vacuum will be created, because with the destruction of Soviet airborne divisions and armies on the fields and mountains of Israel (Ezekiel 39:4-5), the chronic problem for Israel with the Arab enemies will also be solved militarily and politically. Finally, Israel can breath freely and it can expand, and Jerusalem can begin to grow again unhindered. (We hope that the Lord will let us experience this great vacuum here on earth when Israel shall be enlarged in spite of the fact that we are yearning for the Rapture!)

The development or result of the short and

terrible happenings of World War III will accelerate the establishment of the Roman World Empire, which will center in Rome with united Europe and a worldwide alliance from the Far East and the Middle East, including the U.S.A. and Canada.

Now, the time has come that this strong superman, who will take the destiny of the nations of the world in his hands, will be revealed, but before this happens, the Rapture must take place. This time period is the most dangerous one for Israel! It is the time of which the Scripture speaks, *"For when they shall say, Peace and safety; then sudden destruction cometh upon them, as travail upon a woman with child; and they shall not escape"* (I Thessalonians 5:3). At the same time, this is the period when Jerusalem, according to Revelation 11:8 , is called *Sodom and Gomorrah*. We must keep in mind, however, that before this super-human or beast, the lawless one called the Antichrist, can fully reveal himself, we, the Church of Jesus, must be taken away from the earth. And because these events are about to happen at any moment, it is high time to be absolutely involved in watching, praying, and living in total surrender and holiness. This is absolutely essential for every child of God today!

To look back at the fulfillment of Ezekiel 38 and 39, which we are experiencing right now, it is very noteworthy to see how the Soviet Union is almost being forced by invisible powers to arm themselves beyond any possible need.

"Russia is unhinderingly building its military power systematically without stop. Its effectiveness has been proven to the entire world through its brutal invasion of Afghanistan. Western military experts name three examples: 1) The airborne divisions and potential of the Soviet army, which was used in the occupation of Afghanistan is constantly being enlarged. Over 80 of the gigantic jets called I-76, capable of carrying over 40 tons of material, are at the disposal of the army. The Soviet civil air line (Aeroflot) which also uses these planes can, if needed, quickly be converted for military purposes. 2) Each and every month, the Soviet Union is producing 30 attack helicopters. It is estimated that the Warsaw Pact will have at its disposal more than 1,000 MI-24 attack helicopters. They are equipped with 30 millimeter machine guns and cannons, and laser guided equipment for its fire power is on each machine. The attack helicopters of the MI-24 type are equiped with 4 anti-tank missiles, are capable of firing 64 air-ground missiles, and have the capacity to carry 3 tons. 3) In the Soviet Union, every single day, 7 medium to heavy tanks are produced, and yearly, 1,000 tank vehicles are produced."

Another report says the following:

"The Soviet fear of a possible conflict with the U.S.A. has been decreasing substantially and they obviously have taken advantage of the weakness of this super-power and have turned it quickly to the advantage of Russia. It is certainly the end of the previous so-called stabilization and equal power distribution of these two world powers. A new era in world politics has begun which will result in either the absolute superiority of the Soviets or a new World War."

Many today, seem to overlook the fact that Iran, which at the time of this writing, is not yet occupied by Soviet troops, but is strongly and above all expectations undermined by Communists. The following statement was broadcast by the National French Radio on December 21, 1979 and confirmed by a niece of the Shah: "The Revolutionaries who occupy the U.S. Embassy, first of all, flew the red flag! That was witnessed by all of us." To the question, "Are there any agents of Moscow under the Khomeini government?" The Princess answers, "Yes, for instance, the foreign minister, Ghotbzadeh is one, but the most important Communist agents are to be found under the Moslem clergy. That I'd like to emphasize especially." "The military," according to the opinion of the Shah's niece, "became easy prey for the Communist ideology in the face of the weakening West and the chaos in their own country. Thus, a National Communist Ideology was quickly formed."

The most dangerous thing for unconverted people today, consists of the decreasing ability to believe in the truth of the Bible, because this ability is being decreased in the same measure that the prophecy is being fulfilled today! In other words, in the same measure we optically witness that the Word of God is, in reality, the truth; the inner ability to believe decreases.

This is a tremendous and serious warning, for even though man sees, he is not able to believe that which he does not see. And that too, is judgment for today. From that fact, we understand the parallel of the increasing fulfillment of Biblical prophecy, and at the same time, the hardening and rejection of it by people everywhere. It is also exactly what Jesus said in Luke 18:8, *"when the Son of man cometh, shall he find faith on the earth?"* This too, for a true follower of Jesus, is a reason for an increasing and greater joy, because all of these things clearly and unmistakably prove the fulfilling of Biblical prophecy. But for those who are outside of Christ, it only hardens their hearts more and is judgment for them, just as it was in olden times. Remember, the more Pharaoh visibly witnessed the judgments and miracles of God, the more his heart hardened. Therefore, receive today the warning of the Lord: *"Today if ye will hear his voice, Harden not your hearts"* (Hebrews 3:7-8). The Lord is coming soon!

# By The Same Author

**Biblical Counseling**     Wim Malgo
Contains original letters from people in search of a Scriptual answer to a variety of needs. Great help for Ministers, Counselors, Teachers, and every serious Christian. Very interesting and informative, this book makes an ideal gift for any occasion. Order extra copies today!    **$3.95**

1 book: $3.95; 2 books: $6.00; 3 books: $8.00

**Begin with Sadat**     Wim Malgo
This book shows in clear biblical terms the prophetic significance of Egypt's relationship with Israel and its role in God's Eternal plan of salvation. The author also shows that true Christians are actually involved in the Middle East dispute. You will want to read this exciting book immediately.

**Israel's Last Son**     Wim Malgo
Illuminating Benjamin's life reveals to us some amazing facts so often over-looked. This book has a special blesing for every reader.

## ISRAEL'S GOD DOES NOT LIE
### by Wim Malgo                                    $3.95

This book is a must for every serious Christian, who is waiting for the Second Coming of Christ. The Author penetrates deeply into the Spiritual background of the latest events in the Middle East, including the "Yom Kippur War". Illuminating these events in the light of Bible Prophecy, many astonishing truths are clearly revealed as never before.

Some of the Chapters contained in this book ● The Yom Kippur War ● Jerusalem's Border ● Will the Antichrist come from the tribe of Dan? ● The Destruction of the Nations ● The First and the Last King of Jerusalem . . . and more.

**1 book $3.95**                          **2 books $5.00**

**4 books $10.00**

## 1000 YEARS PEACE . . . A UTOPIA?
### by Wim Malgo                                    $2.95

A refreshing outline on the much debated subject; the millennium. Without discussion and argument the author goes direct to the source; the Bible, to show the clear teaching of the coming 1000 years peace. The millennium is the answer to Jesus' prayer "Thy Kingdom Come." The patriarchs, prophets, kings and priests looked forward to the thousand year reign of peace.
Some of the chapters in this book: Israel's position in the millennium . . . Where will the church be during the millennium? . . . What will happen after the millennium? . . . etc.

**1 book $2.95**                          **2 books $5.00**

**3 books $7.00**

## THE LAST DAYS
### by Wim Malgo $2.95

Each day the Church is drawing closer to the day when the "fullness of the Gentiles be come in" which will climax into the RAPTURE of all born-again believers. This book gives a clear biblical answer to why the battle in the invisible world is the reason for the near-chaos condition of the world today.

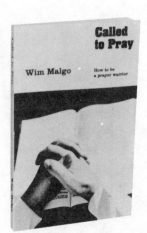

## CALLED TO PRAY
### by Wim Malgo $2.95

An enlightening and reliable guidance to a victorious prayer-life. Read in this book how Prophets, Apostles, Priests and Kings used PRAYER to overcome the enemy. Tells how your life in Christ can become a powerful testimony. PRAYER is one of the most important subjects in your Bible. 17 INSPIRING CHAPTERS TO FILL YOUR HEART. A REAL TREASURE IN EVERY CHRISTIAN HOME.

**1 book $2.95**                    **2 books $5.00**

**3 books $7.00**

## SHADOWS OF ARMAGEDDON

**by Wim Malgo** $3.95
What began in 1948 in the Middle East as a seemingly insignificant local matter has taken on world-wide proportions today. The Author shows in unmistakably clear terms that even political conflicts such as Vietnam and Cyprus are definitely signs of the preparation for the battle of Armageddon.

## SEVEN SIGNS OF A BORN AGAIN PERSON

**by Wim Malgo** 95c
A crystal clear outline how to recognize a truly born-again person. Answers vital questions every one should know.
SEVEN BIBLICAL SIGNS

## PRAYER AND REVIVAL

**by Wim Malgo** $3.95
What can we do to cause a Revival? How does a Revival begin? Does God want to send a Revival? There are divine conditions we must first meet in order to have Revival. Analyzing these conditions for Revival through the Bible, this book will help serious Christians to find the pathway to Revival.

## THE RAPTURE

**by Wim Malgo** 95c

This booklet gives light on . . . How will it happen? . . . who will take part? . . . what must I do? . . . and many other important questions answered.

VALUABLE FOR BIBLE STUDY

## Israel Shall Do Valiantly

**by Wim Malgo** $2.95

A book which makes Prophecy come alive! Over 3400 years ago it was said: "Israel Shall Do Valiantly" today this Prophecy has become a visible reality in the Middle East. Wim Malgo expounds biblically the Holy Land and it's people from the old past to the present and into the future. Israel, the uncomparable and most astonishing nation of this century. Some of the chapters in this book include . . . Israel's origin, calling, tragedy and future . . . Russia's miscalculation and Israel . . . The connection between space travel, nuclear threat and Israel . . . Is the Antichrist already among us? . . . The last two witnesses before world wide catastrophe . . . and other vital subjects.

**1 book $2.95** **2 books $5.00**

**3 books $7.00**

## ON THE BORDER OF TWO WORLDS

**by Wim Malgo** 95c

Tells how a Christian can keep the victory in his daily walk with Christ. Subjects included: In Enemy Territory . . . The Great WHY . . . Religious Deception . . . False Spirits . . . Demonic Bonds . . . Victory in Everyday Life . . . and more.

# ORDER FORM

*Fill in, Clip, and Mail this Whole Page to:*

**MIDNIGHT CALL   P.O. Box 864   Columbia, SC 29202**

| How Many | Title | Total Price |
|---|---|---|
| _____ | Russia's Last Invasion ........................$2.95 | _____ |
| _____ | Shadows of Armageddon ....................$3.95 | _____ |
| _____ | There Shall Be Signs From 1948 to 1982 .....$2.95 | _____ |
| _____ | Prayer and REvival ..........................$3.95 | _____ |
| _____ | The Last Days ..............................$2.95 | _____ |
| _____ | Jerusalem Focal Point of the World ..........$2.95 | _____ |
| _____ | Israel's God Does Not Lie ..................$3.95 | _____ |
| _____ | 1000 Years Peace ..........................$2.95 | _____ |
| _____ | Israel Shall Do Valiantly ....................$2.95 | _____ |
| _____ | Called To Pray .............................$2.95 | _____ |
| _____ | The Rapture .................................$.95 | _____ |
| _____ | Seven Signs of a Born-Again Person ..........$.95 | _____ |
| _____ | Terrifying Goal of Ecumenical Movement......$.95 | _____ |
| _____ | On The Border of Two Worlds ................$.95 | _____ |
| _____ | Group Dynamics, New Tool of the Antichrist ..$.95 | _____ |
| _____ | Signs and Wonders ..........................$.95 | _____ |
| _____ | Begin with Sadat............................$1.95 | _____ |
| _____ | Biblical Counseling .........................$3.95 | _____ |
| _____ | How to Walk With God .......................$.95 | _____ |

Please enclose $4.00 for a one-year subscription to each of the following publications:

☐ MIDNIGHT CALL Magazine     ☐ NEWS FROM ISRAEL

TOTAL ENCLOSED: _____

**Mr.**
NAME.**Mrs.**_____
**Miss**
ADDRESS_____

CITY_____ STATE_____ ZIP_____

Dear Friend in Christ,

This book, RUSSIA'S LAST INVASION--
I am sending to you with an inner
assurance that its message will be of
great help to you and your loved ones.

I realize that you have not ordered
this book, but because of the urgency of
the times we live in, I am sending it to
each reader of MIDNIGHT CALL. By doing
so, we are saving a tremendous amount of
money on postage and handling by not
having to pack and mail each individual
order.

Furthermore, the end-time message of
this book must be published as far and
wide as possible, and only you, our
reader can help us achieve this goal.
Therefore, please read this book prayer-
fully and permit the message to become a
decisive blessing for your life. Then
be sure to order extra copies for your
relatives, friends, and neighbors.

The cost of this book is $2.95 plus
.80¢ for postage and handling. If in
any way you can help to defray this
cost, we will greatly appreciate it.
Attached is a self-addressed postage-
paid envelope for your convenience.

The Lord bless you richly,

Wim Malgo

Dear Dr. Malgo,

I am enclosing my gift to help carry the cost of sending forth the Word of God through your Worldwide Ministry.

☐ $5    ☐ $10    ☐ $20    ☐ $30    ☐ $50

☐ $100    ☐ $_____

## I wish my gift to be used for:

☐ Radio Ministry (covers 90% of Communist countries)
☐ Beth Shalom (Israel)          ☐ Literature Distribution
☐ Missionary Training Institute    ☐ Hospital Work
☐ Missionary Work               ☐ General Fund
☐ Jungle Orphanage             ☐ Where Needed Most

---

**You may also help distribute some extra copies of this important book . We have made arrangements for special low prices when ordered in quantities.**

---

☐ Please send me additional copies of your book
*Russia's Last Invasion*

☐   2 books    $   5.00
☐   5 books    $ 10.00      Total enclosed for Gift $_____
☐  10 books    $ 18.00
☐  20 books    $ 30.00      Total enclosed for books $_____
☐  50 books    $ 60.00
☐ 100 books    $100.00          Total Enclosed $_____

Name _____

Street _____

City _____ State_____ Zip_____